Niacin Can Curb Craving For Alcohol

Niacin Can Curb Craving For Alcohol

BERNARD D. ROSS, M.D., Ph.D.

**MANCORP
PUBLISHING**

Tampa, Florida

Copyright © 1990 by Bernard D. Ross

All rights reserved.

Typesetting: Presentation Graphics

Printed in the United States of America

Library of Congress Cataloging-in-Publication Data

Ross, Bernard D., 1916-
    Niacin can curb craving for alcohol.

    Includes bibliographical references.
    1. Alcoholism   2. Niacin.
I. Title.
RC565.R568   1990   616.86'1061   89-13738
ISBN 0-931541-16-6

DEDICATION:

To the memory of my father, Daniel Ross, D.D.S.

ACKNOWLEDGEMENTS:

I wish to express my thanks to my step-daughter, Deirdre Sewell, and to Mrs. Marilyn Heinstein, who typed the manuscript and to Dr. Gwen Morgan for her valuable copyediting.

STATEMENT FROM THE PUBLISHER

I met Dr. Bernard D. Ross in 1983 after reviewing a manuscript describing his optimal dose therapy. His assertions were so intriguing, with far reaching implications, that I proceeded to investigate.

Dr. Ross comes with solid credentials having received his education at M.I.T. and at the University of Chicago where he was awarded the M.D. and Ph.D. degrees. His background in research, and practice as a primary care physician since 1944, attest to his high degree of accomplishments.

Over the years, the medical profession has spent millions of dollars and many man-hours trying to conquer muscular dystrophy, but to no avail. Dr. Ross' treatment of patients with this debilitating disease seems to be offering a ray of hope. He has invited the Muscular Dystrophy Association to participate in his studies.

In this book, Dr. Ross describes his work with individuals suffering from alcoholism. To the millions who suffer from alcohol addiction this book presents a remarkable treatment, and to the medical profession it offers a challenge to investigate the effects of niacin and Dr. Ross' method of therapy.

M.N. Manougian, Ph.D.

CONTENTS

Foreward — xi

Chapter One — Introduction — 1

Chapter Two — Is Medicine Truly a Science? — 11

Chapter Three — IRT and the Scourge of the Ages — 27

Chapter Four — The End of the Rainbow is in Sight — 63

Chapter Five — A 60 Mile Mission of Mercy to Deliver 4.5 Milligrams of Niacin — 73

Chapter Six — Niacin — Therapeutic Superstar — 85

Chapter Seven — Injectable Niacin is Not for Sale — 105

Epilogue — 111

Appendix — 117

Bibliography — 125

FOREWARD

The purpose of this book is:

1. To present a method which will consistently curb or dissipate a craving for alcohol in people who suffer from *alcoholism.*

2. To present evidence that this method is successful even though it employs a therapeutic item, injectable niacin, which has been discarded by the medical profession after years of use as being relatively worthless.

3. To present evidence that this method is effective in producing the results noted above only when ad-

ministered by a new and original technique *Individualized Replacement Therapy* (IRT).

4. To present evidence that injectable niacin can also be of significant therapeutic benefit in patients suffering from a variety of other medical conditions, including *muscular dystrophy*, if it is administered by the same technique (IRT). Such results have never previously been reported from the administration of niacin by *any technique whatsoever*.

Chapter One

INTRODUCTION

*A*LTHOUGH MY APPOINTMENT schedule was somewhat swelled by emergencies, I waited with pleasant anticipation for my next patient, a physician who was an admitted alcoholic. He entered my consultation room to take his seat and smiled as he responded to my questions regarding the two minute vitamin injections I had administered to him during the previous four weeks.

"My craving for alcohol, which had been present since my teens, subsided completely within 24 hours after I received the first five-milligram injection of niacin, four weeks ago. It remained absent during the first week, but then it returned to some extent during the second week, when you gave me an identical injection. After the second injection, which I received two weeks ago, I am glad to tell you that the desire again disappeared completely and has not recurred during the entire two-week period since I saw you last." Following this conversation, which occurred on July 22, 1986, I administered a third five-milligram injection of niacin. At this time we did not make a definite appointment for another follow-up visit, but I did advise the patient to phone me if and when his craving for alcohol recurred.

I have since talked to this physician, from time to time, during the course of every day professional activity. On each occasion his message has been as definite as ever: "The craving has not recurred as yet!" He happily delivered his most recent such report to me by telephone on March 15, 1989, almost three years after he had received his third minidose of niacin.

The reader should know that the alcoholic to whom I have been referring is a personal friend and an accomplished surgeon who has practiced medicine in our community for many years. He did not hesitate to remind me that the remarkable sequence of events just described was making medical history, for it has never previously been reported that any therapeutic agent curbed a person's desire for alcohol. Moreover, the very idea that a series of only three miniscule injections, each containing a mere five milligrams of niacin and spaced as far apart as two weeks, could have any noticeable or lasting effect is completely incomprehensible in the light of currently accepted principles governing niacin or any other vitamin required by the human body.

After repeated success in helping to curb or dissipate alcohol by administering minidoses of niacin, I felt it appropriate to write this book for interested laymen as well as physicians. It should be mentioned that the present book is a sequel to my first, *The Fundamental Pathway to Better Health*, which describes and discusses fully the new and original method of minidose vitamin and hormone therapy, which I have termed *Individualized Replacement Therapy* (IRT). This second book describes the remarkable benefits which can accrue from the use of IRT as exemplified by niacin. I am reasonably sure that by the time the reader finishes this book, he will agree with my classification of niacin as the *forgotten vitamin.*

Any one with a basic knowledge of nutrition or biology will recognize that a five-milligram dose of niacin is minute when it is compared to the commonly used oral doses of as much as 2000 mg which are often employed to control blood cholesterol levels on a daily basis. At the end of a two week period, daily ingestion of such 2000 mg doses would result in introducing a total of 28,000 mg of niacin into the body. Routine arithmetic may lead us to conclude that a daily dose of 2000 mg of niacin, if tolerated by the recipient, should be far more effective than a dose of five mg over a period of two weeks or longer. It should be noted, moreover, that an average diet which people eat in the United States today probably contains a daily quantity of niacin which the FDA estimates to be at least twenty mg daily. If this were not so, doctors would still frequently encounter cases of pellagra, a deficiency disease, which tends to occur in people who ingest less than the twenty mg of niacin, which the FDA estimates to be the minimum daily requirement of the human body. That pellagra has been virtually non-existent in the United States for decades (most doctors in medical practice today have never seen a case) is evidence that the requirement is being met through normal eating practices.

Current thinking, therefore, would lead us to believe that, if niacin were as an effective treatment for alcoholism as it is for pellagra, alcoholism should be virtually non-existent, for the required niacin would be ingested in the diet of most people, as noted above.

It should also be mentioned, moreover, that many Americans supplement the twenty mg of niacin contained in their daily diets with that contained in certain multi-vitamin capsules or potent niacin tablets used for cholesterol control. In other words, virtually everybody in the United States whose diet is not restricted to maize corn would be protected against alcoholism if niacin counteracted that disease and standard arithmetical principles prevailed. But alcoholism *does indeed exist* as a major medical problem in our society, just as surely as niacin mini-injections are successful in treating cases such as I have described. Therefore, it is obvious that more is involved in the relationship between niacin and alcoholism than mere mathematical calculations.

Logical analysis produces only one apparent answer to this enigmatic situation. The niacin alone being insufficient, the *unique method* whereby the niacin was administered to those whose craving for alcohol was controlled so effectively, must be essential to successful treatment.

Until they accept and learn to use IRT in terms of injectable niacin, frustrated doctors still can do little more than treat victims of alcoholism in detoxification and in sanitariums, using kind words, education, the appropriate tranquilizing drugs, and the necessary psychiatric consultations. And, to make matters even worse, any apparent success with such therapy is usually only temporary. Relapses are the rule with alcoholism and tend to come and go over the entire lifetime of an afflicted individual.

This bleak picture explains why the average physician is anything but enthused by the arrival in his office of a patient who is honest enough to admit that he has an irresistible need for intoxicants such as wine, beer, whiskey, vodka or, perhaps, champagne. The term "honest" is used advisedly, for it has long been known that victims of alcoholism tend to deny the existence of their problem not only to others, but even to themselves. I must admit, therefore, that for many years I treated each victim of alcoholism with the feeling that I was merely wasting his time as well as my own. Nevertheless, I struggled along with each patient, doing the best I could, for I realized that I was the responsible physician to whom he had come for help, as meager as that help may be.

Over the years, however, my attitude began to change. I began to look forward with pleasant anticipation to treating patients whose histories even minimally suggested that they ever had problems with alcoholism at any time in their past. Why did my attitude change so drastically? Those who have read the opening paragraphs in this introduction will logically conclude that it has something to do with the use of niacin as a therapeutic agent in the treatment of patients with alcoholism.

Chapter Two

IS MEDICINE TRULY A SCIENCE?

We must endeavor to understand the significance of IRT in the broad expanse of modern medical knowledge before we can comprehend its significance in the treatment of alcoholism and a variety of other diseases. This is necessary because, as it took me many years to realize, medical practice in this "modern" era is characterized by a marked and fundamental inadequacy which has escaped the recognition of others, who, I feel I can prove, have failed to "see the forest for the trees."

In this chapter I will lay the groundwork to show, step by step, a marked deficiency in medical thinking which can adequately be replaced by a system of therapy such as IRT, therapy that can logically be expected to promote medical progress. As I proceed, I believe I can prove to the interested reader that the only method of therapy which could logically be expected to achieve the type of results this book describes, even with regard to different and apparently unrelated medical problems, would necessarily be IRT or a very similar method possessing some other name.

Most laymen I have encountered during my 44 years of medical practice are completely convinced that medicine is necessarily a science. To them, and to most physicians, it seems rather obvious that any branch of learning which has developed such remarkable technological developments such as CT Scans, Magnetic Image Resonance, Laser Beam surgery, and organ transplants, not to mention a growing armament of life-saving antibiotics and cardiac drugs, must necessarily be quite scientific. Is such an assumption valid? To answer this question, we must first carefully review the basic features of any field of knowledge which permit it to be classified as a science. One fundamental requirement is that it be universal in nature and be completely constant in its theories, principles and underlying characteristics, regardless of the geographical location in which it is practiced or the language through which it is communicated. In other words, it does not matter whether we are in New York, in London, or on the Great Wall of China. It does not matter whether one is a Frenchman visiting the United States or a German tourist in Italy. The solution of a mathematical equation in algebra, calculus, or trigonometry, for example, is always the same regardless of who is solving the problem or where the solver happens to be at the time. Does the field of medicine comply with this simple stipulation? The answer to this question is not hard to find. In a recent article (see Reference 3) which appeared in MD in January 1986, Lynn Payer, a medical writer who has been covering medical meetings for sixteen years, described results of her studies of the way medicine is practiced in various countries of Europe. Excerpts of her interesting report are reproduced below.

"Anybody who has ever been to a medical meeting in a foreign country knows that medicine is not quite the international science it's often made out to be. Even if the simultaneous translation is accurate, the translated words often seem meaningless. As one Finnish doctor put it: 'At a meeting, the Finns tend to group with the English. The Germans stay together in a block, as do the Southern and Eastern

Europeans. I seldom talk with the French. I'm half sleepy whenever French is spoken.' And at smaller meetings, where communication is better, one is apt to hear such comments as 'We would not do that in our country,' or 'That would be malpractice at home!'"

"In the past two decades, attempts have been made to document differences in surgery rates, drug consumption, and diagnoses in various countries of Western Europe and North America, and the magnitude of differences has often surprised even those most familiar with medicine in the countries concerned. In German-speaking countries, the appendectomy rate is roughly three times what it is elsewhere. The United States has twice as much surgery overall as England, although half as much psychosurgery. German doctors consider fatigue without other symptoms a sure sign of cardiac insufficiency and, as a consequence, prescribe about seven times per capita the amounts of digoxin and nitroglycerin as their colleagues in England and France. Until recently, the French had 300 different drugs for the liver, which they prescribed for what is vernacularly known as *'liver crisis'*: and the German equivalent of the *Physicians' Desk Reference* lists 85 drugs for the treatment of low blood pressure." It is important to note that *Physicians' Desk Reference* does not mention even one prescription drug for the treatment of low blood pressure in the United States.

"Concern over fertility also makes the French extremely hesitant to perform hysterectomies. Indeed, hysterectomy, the most commonly performed major operation in the United States, was not even listed in a recent ranking of the most frequent surgical procedures in France."

"...the diagnosis that's really been sweeping France is spasmophilia. The disease, which is diagnosed by a positive Chvostek's sign and abnormal electromyogram, and treated with either calcium or magnesium, increased sevenfold between 1970 and 1980. 'I've seen thousands of cases here,' remarked Dr. Jean Durlach, one of the disorder's French proponents, 'and I think about six cases have been reported in American medical literature.'"

Miss Payer provides a very explicit answer regarding the first pre-requisite of science: medicine is definitely not universal. By this fact alone, it is immediately obvious that the claim of the field of medicine as a science is dubious.

More fundamental is the question as to whether medicine, as it is practiced by most physicians, complies with the basic law of science and logic to which all of the traditionally natural sciences completely adhere: the principle of cause and effect. This is based upon the axiomatic principle that an observation cannot be classified as being truly "scientific" if it depends upon the introduction of more than one new factor at the same time in any problem situation. This is true because any procedure which ignores this basic principle defies all efforts to make a logical analysis of the results which are observed. How well does the field of medicine meet this basic requirement? During the more than four decades in which I have been engaged in medical practice I have rarely, if ever, seen a physician who takes the time and trouble to avoid giving a patient a multiplicity of new prescriptions and/or a variety of advice regarding changes in lifestyle during the course of one visit. The following example is typical of this situation.

"You need longer rest periods every day. You should eat less salt and less sugar in your diet. You should drink more water and try to avoid situations which might cause any nervous or physical strain.

And be sure to get these prescriptions filled for Lanoxin, Lasix and Dalmane. And, finally, it would not hurt to use Metamucil for your constipation and to start on a good multiple vitamin preparation such as Centrum. On your way out, the nurse will make an appointment for a follow-up visit."

The above is an example of routine treatment for a patient with a heart problem not severe enough to require hospitalization, and is currently acceptable in any typical medical office. If we translate what the doctor in this situation has ordered into simple arithmetic, we find that he has introduced six changes in lifestyle, four new drugs and a vitamin capsule containing 30 different ingredients. This adds up to a total of 40 different factors which the doctor hopes, and expects, will help his patient to improve.

A little careful thought will lead us to conclude that this procedure cannot conceivably permit the doctor to make a valid appraisal of the factor or factors which might be responsible for any changes he observes in his patient when he returns two weeks later. Perhaps all he needed was more rest. Perhaps only a change in his diet, in terms of sugar or salt, or perhaps he merely needed the Lanoxin which had been prescribed. The doctor obviously cannot begin to know specifically why his patient improved, or in less fortunate circumstances, became even sicker.

Why does this physician continue this same type of routine treatment day after day, even though it obviously does not comply with the basic law of cause and effect? And why does the typical physician continue such a practice, and with apparent success? There are several overlapping reasons. Primarily, he does so because medical textbooks and lectures fail to include any significant discussion of the fact that the multiple procedures considered correct treatments for a particular disease should not be started all at the same time.

How can an average physician practice medicine successfully in such an obviously unscientific fashion throughout his entire career? There must be a reason for this puzzling situation, for there is no other occupation or profession in which consistent success can be expected by an individual who deliberately introduces 40 different factors into a problem situation at the same time.

After many years of careful thinking, I have arrived at what I believe to be a satisfactory solution to this puzzling question. The solution lies in the fact that an experienced physician is a competent statistician who is able to use empiricism effectively because he is working with a deck of cards which is consistently "stacked" in his favor. This is true because he is always dealing with a self-repairing machine. In other words, he routinely takes advantage of the repeated observation that 50-70% of all patients who visit doctors' offices will probably get well, regardless of the affliction suffered or the treatment which a particular doctor prescribes.

Empiricism, according to *Webster's Unabridged Dictionary*, is a school of medical practice which is based upon experience rather than upon science or theory. This definition appears snugly to fit the attitude of the average physician, like a well made glove, for he obviously does not approach a problem scientifically, but rather bases his methodology upon experience and statistics. Each experienced physician thereby learns to use statistics instead of science in a routine fashion to get satisfactory results, day after day. He uses a variety of therapeutic maneuvers, each of which he knows, from experience, will usually be helpful. Since he is successful most of the time, he sees no reason to question the true value of each type of medication or advice he prescribes for each patient. After all, what speaks louder than success? Why bother with academic considerations such as scientific theory?

This type of thinking appears all too frequently in hospital records. I recall, for example, an incident which occurred several years ago when I questioned, at a local hospital, an order written by a leading surgeon in our community to have a patient receive two different hormone injections at the same time. His immediate and emphatic reply still rings in my ears: "You should know, Dr. Ross, that this is not a scientific project. This is the way we practice medicine." Such a response definitely was not the statement of a scientist, but an unthinking announcement that the physician was an empiricist whose practice of medicine was based upon experience rather than upon science or theory.

Another example is that of a cardiologist who is well known in his community for his scholarship and professional accomplishments. I learned about his usual procedure from a woman who was employed as a ward clerk in the coronary care unit of the hospital in which he practiced. It was her responsibility to process the orders written by the various attending physicians concerning the details of various forms of therapy prescribed for specific patients. This lady confidentially informed me that the cardiologist, who often would see severely ill heart patients on consultation, routinely and repeatedly proceeded in the same empirical fashion I have been discussing. If a patient had been taking six different medications, for example, he did not hesitate to discontinue all six of them and replace them by six different ones at one and the same time.

I do not see how any one can claim that this admittedly brilliant, well-trained and accomplished physician is a person dedicated to scientific principles. If such an outstanding medical scholar practices his profession in this empirical fashion, what can be expected of the average physician who does not have this specialist's "blue ribbon" rating? The answer should be obvious. I contend, therefore, that medicine is not a true science and that most practicing physicians are not really scientists, and I do not believe that my contention can be readily refuted.

Before completing this chapter, I wish to make clear that the complexities of medical practice do not always permit strict adherence to the law of cause and effect. A common example is the presence of an acute, life-threatening emergency. On such occasions, compromises must be made because time is of the essence, and the empirical approach may be absolutely essential to save the life of the patient. Nevertheless it is equally necessary I believe, for the physician to be fully aware that he is deliberately compromising his scientific principles because specific circumstances require it. If he can do so successfully, then and only then can such a physician be classified as a scientist.

One may ask, "What difference does it really make? After all an empiricist also gets good results, doesn't he?" It actually makes a tremendous difference. Those physicians who follow faithfully the trail of true science can learn more and more from each experience in which they administer one therapeutic item as a time. By doing so, they can appreciate more fully the true value of each component of the therapeutic armament upon which the practice of medicine depends. Through continued empiricism, on the other hand, physicians really learn nothing from each additional experience, regardless of the number of years they have been in active practice.

In keeping with my beliefs regarding the nature of scientific medicine, I am proud to say I have strictly adhered to the scientific method in my daily practice for 40 years. I have consequently made approximately 150,000 truly scientific observations since 1949, learning more each day about scientific forms of therapy and specific drugs. A major result of my efforts was the new form of therapy I devised and have mentioned above, which I term *Individualized Replacement Therapy* (IRT), and which can supplement all currently acceptable forms of medical therapy. It is described fully in my previous book *The Fundamental Pathway to Better Health*, and I contend that it represents the most fundamental form of therapy we can conceive at this time. Here, I can ask the same question I asked in that earlier book: "What could be more fundamental than the precise replacement of the exact ingredients which should have been there in the first place?" If IRT is theoretically and practically correct, its potential should be an unlimited boon to physicians who practice medicine. Moreover, logic dictates that it must necessarily take priority whenever any patient is started on therapy for any disease, unless an emergency or some other practical deterrent is present.

What I wish to emphasize at this time, however, is the fact that I am quite certain that it would have been completely impossible for me to have systematically accumulated the knowledge necessary to formulate the IRT system if I had not steadfastly adhered to the scientific method over the years.

As regards the success of IRT, many of the results I have achieved were described in my previous book. It is my purpose to describe here the additional benefits of IRT with specific application to alcoholism and muscular dystrophy.

Chapter Three

IRT AND THE SCOURGE
OF THE AGES

*I*T IS WITH HUMILITY THAT the author presents this chapter as a promise of hope to the many victims of alcohol and, perhaps, drugs such as cocaine and marijuana. Countless books have been written and sermons have been preached regarding the destructive effects of alcohol, which may rightly be termed the "Scourge of the Ages."

Even as we approach the advent of the twenty-first century, all the remarkable technological advances in medicine the world has seen continue to fail in reducing the negative impact of alcohol upon the peoples of the world. But a ray of light, IRT, is now visible on the horizon and appears to have the potential to illuminate this and other murky areas in the world of medicine. In the treatment of patients with alcoholism, IRT chiefly employs *niacin* as the specific agent, as was mentioned in my introduction.

It must be stressed that niacin, although accepted for decades as the anti-pellagra vitamin and generally available as oral tablets, is relatively worthless in the treatment of alcoholism unless it is administered in the form of *individualized precisely measured injections*, in accordance with the principles of IRT. As was dramatically exemplified in the case of the physician discussed in the introduction, this proper use of niacin provides us, for the first time, with an effective and safe physical weapon which can curb a person's craving for alcohol.

So far I have observed that the use of niacin injections has been effective, to varying degrees, in curbing or dissipating completely the craving for alcohol in a majority of people to whom I have administered it by the IRT method. Before discussing the details of the specific procedure employed in my niacin treatment of a series of alcoholics, it seems appropriate to present copies of three letters, written by two of the subjects to be described below. The first two were written by Mr. J. Calvin Peace, a minister who is also a qualified counsellor in alcoholism. The third was written by Richard B. Allen, M.D., a physician who had a problem with cocaine as well as alcohol.

A Better Way In Christ Rescue Mission
304 N. 12th Street • Fort Pierce, Florida 33448

April 26, 1987

To Whom It May Concern:

Dr. Bernard Ross has been treating me and a number of other alcoholics from the Rescue Mission I have operated in Fort Pierce, Florida for the past five years.

Every two weeks we meet with Dr. Ross and at that time receive a vitamin injection. I have known most of these men for a number of years and have witnessed a dramatic change in their lives. None of us who have continued the injections have had a drink of alcohol, or had a desire for alcohol since we started with Dr. Ross. Several of the men have gone far beyond their "normal" dry period and still have not had a drink. In addition, our bodies are more relaxed and our health in general seems to be improving.

I am very enthused over Dr. Ross' medical discovery and in my many years as a writer and editor for daily newspapers, I have never uncovered anything as remarkable as this, nor anything that has the potential of helping more people than this does.

Sincerely your,

J. Calvin Peace, Director

A Better Way In Christ Rescue Mission
304 N. 12th Street • Fort Pierce, Florida 33448

Oct. 27, 1987

Dr. Bernard D. Ross
885 E. Prima Vista Blvd.
Pt. St. Lucie, FL 33452

Dear Dr. Ross:

I will be at your office tonight on time with all the men, and looking forward to it. I think I just fully realized today how much your treatment has really meant to me.

I don't think anyone fully realizes what a strain and the stress I have been under since Mary's illness developed in June. I have worked almost 16 hours a day, 7 days a week for months. I cook all of the meals at home and see that Mary is fed. I clean her "halo" screws in her skull twice a day, see that she is medicated four times a day; do all of the bookwork and daily bank deposits for our three stores and our son's two stores and apartment house. I shop for groceries and handle all problems and oversee the Rescue Mission. In addition to answering dozens of phone calls daily and counseling an average of 3 alcoholics daily, and transporting the men for medical help, etc., I also counsel outsiders almost daily who have gotten my name from someone.

In addition, each week, I must prepare my sermon for Sunday morning and deliver it. I then work a full day on Sunday. With a schedule like this, I have not caved in and I feel great and sleep well. I just realized that it has to be your treatment that is responsible. The majority of alcoholics would have long ago caved in. Thank you for everything!

We will see you tonight at 7 p.m.

I also need a favor from you (see attached sheet). Thanks again for everything!

Sincerely yours,

J. Calvin Peace, Director

RICHARD B. ALLEN, M.D.
Otolaryngology • Ear • Nose • Throat
1801 S.E. Hillmoor Drive, Suite B 105
Port St. Lucie, Florida 33452
(305) 879-3506 • (305) 337-0950

November 10, 1987

Bernard Ross, M.D.
885 E. Prima Vista Blvd.
Port St. Lucie, Fl. 34952

Dear Dr. Ross,

    I want to take a moment and thank you for your personal care as my physician and the opportunity to participate in your Niacin study. As you recall, in March of this year, I returned from alcoholism and drug addiction treatment. Over the last eight months, I have been treated by you with Niacin replacement therapy according to your protocol. Initially, I was under a tremendous amount of stress and felt that the Niacin injections would be of no benefit but was willing to undergo the treatment with the possibility of any kind of help. With the initiation of the first dose I had physical symptoms of a tremendous headache on what I considered a micro dose of Niacin. I was surprised at this finding as well as the increase in my energy level, the improvement in the handling of my stress and the overall feeling of well being. As I stated to you I felt that I went from a 60% feeling of energy and coping to 100% which lasted approximately two to three weeks. With the adjustment of the dose and continued injections I have been able to go approximately six weeks. When I extend this beyond that to eight to ten weeks, I do notice a definite change in my stress response and my general feeling. At this point, I truly believe *that the addition of the Niacin therapy to the rest of my support and recovery environment has aided greatly in my continued recovery and my relief from my obsessions.*

Again, I want to thank you for your help and consideration and hope that this may prove to be of substantial benefit to others with similar problems.

Sincerely,

Richard B. Allen, M.D.

I feel that these letters are effective testimony to the beneficial effects of niacin upon people who have a problem with alcoholism. The letter from the physician, moreover, indicates that niacin may be helpful in the treatment of people who have a problem with cocaine as well as with alcohol. It also should not be overlooked that these letters indicate that niacin does much more than act as a drug which serves the isolated function of curbing a craving for alcohol, and perhaps, other intoxicants. As a vitamin, and a vital ingredient of all living tissues of the human body, its administration in carefully calibrated, optimal doses, serves to improve the treatment. As a result, every component part of the individual including his brain and muscle structure, can be expected to function more effectively, thereby permitting the individual to cope more adequately with all forms of emotional and physical stress.

The author of the first of the above letters, Mr. Peace, estimates that he has been hospitalized between 30-40 times for acute alcoholism. He is, nevertheless, a well-educated and accomplished man who has a college degree in mathematics and has been managing editor of two different newspapers. Despite the fact the he has been living under great stress, as noted in his second letter, he has felt no need for any alcohol for over one year, since he started to receive injections of niacin. In addition, he is consistently aware of a mild dip in his energy level during a period of 24 hours prior to each successive injection. These 5.6 mg doses of niacin are consistently followed within 24 hours by a sensation of increased exhilaration.

The third letter was written by Dr. Allen, a reputable local physician, who found it necessary to close his office for a period of six months to become an in-patient at an alcoholism treatment center in another state. When he began IRT treatments in my office, he had been back to work at his practice for a period of one week. He has been particularly enthusiastic about the results achieved by IRT in his case because he was able to observe and experience the remarkable precision required for the production of desirable therapeutic results with IRT, as noted below.

At the time of his initial injection, I informed this physician that I administered exactly 5.0 mg (0.50 ml of a solution containing 10 mg/ml) of niacin subcutaneously. When he returned for a scheduled follow-up appraisal, two weeks later, he informed me that he had developed a severe, pounding headache within two hours of receiving the injection. The headache lasted for about four hours. For the next two days he experienced his average state of well-being, then sensed a definite improvement in this regard during the subsequent 12 days. When the patient relayed this information, I advised him that it was highly likely that his headache resulted from the magnitude of his niacin dose, which, based on my years of experience with IRT, appeared to be 10% in excess of his optimal dose. In keeping with this, I reduced his second dose from 5.0 to 4.4 mg (0.44 ml of the same solution he had received previously). My prediction that he probably would not experience another headache on this occasion proved to be true.

When the physician returned for his next follow-up visit two weeks later, he reported that he was fully convinced of the validity of IRT. Not only did he feel much better, but the headache did not recur and he still had a much diminished desire for alcohol and cocaine. Nor did he develop a headache after any of the 4.4 mg injections of niacin he had since received over a period of one year. Over this time, the interval between successive injections gradually has been extended to six weeks because of his continued improvement. However, whenever the interval was extended to more than six weeks, he tended to fell shaky and tense. I believe that any open-minded reader who carefully reviews and logically analyzes the data on niacin presented in the Introduction and in this chapter must necessarily come to the following conclusions:

1. Niacin, when administered by small, precisely measured injections, appears consistently to curb the craving for alcohol in patients who have a dependency upon this intoxicant.

2. Niacin produces this effect when administered in far smaller doses (averaging 5 mg every two weeks) than the relatively large ones customarily prescribed by physicians for oral consumption in

the treatment of circulatory problems and elevated blood cholesterol, generally 300 mg or more per day. A remarkable example of the efficacy of small doses of niacin is the case of the physician described in the Introduction, who was still experiencing beneficial effects more than two years subsequent to the administration of three five mg injections of niacin spread over two intervals which were two weeks apart.

Although it undoubtedly would be highly desirable to have my findings corroborated by other investigators, I believe that I have accumulated sufficient information in this area to warrant the presentation of my findings to my fellow physicians and to the lay public in this book.

Why I did not have this material published in a standard medical journal is another matter, which is analyzed in the chapter entitled *"The End of the Rainbow is in Sight"*. This section raises the question as to whether or not scientific studies should be rejected by the editors of reputable medical journals merely because they are not performed under "controlled conditions". At this juncture, it seems appropriate to mention to the reader that controlled studies are used to develop the statistics upon which so many modern physicians rely in their everyday empirical practice of medicine. Under such a system, as was noted in the previous chapter, each patient who walks into a doctor's office merely becomes another statistic in the assembly line of medical treatment. Instead of being treated on an individual basis, he or she receives a combination of different drugs and other forms of therapy, such as diet and changes in lifestyle, which statistics predict will be helpful to the patient. Also pointed out previously was the fact that, under such conditions, a physician can never really be sure of the reasons for any successful results he achieves. In other words, he actually could be ignoring or misinterpreting instance after instance of new therapeutic benefits occurring before his very eyes merely because statistics fail to predict that such benefits would occur. Because he has been doing so many different things at the same time, the doctor could not determine, even if he desired to do so, which factor or factors might have been responsible for any improvement he noticed.

What all this means is that anyone who chiefly relies upon statistics and the controlled studies from which these statistics were derived can never make an independent discovery of any great significance, or appreciate one made by somebody else. This is so because the only discoveries for which his training has truly prepared him are based upon the findings derived from the results of controlled experiments involving large groups of subjects. In contrast, consider the answers to the following questions:

How many times did Mr. Eiffel have to build his tower to prove that he could do so?

How many times did Leonardo da Vinci have to paint the Mona Lisa to prove that he could do so?

How many time did we have to fly a rocket to the moon to prove that we could do so?

The answers to these and a myriad of similar questions are identical: ONCE!

In keeping with this philosophy, I believe that it was necessary for me to prove only *once* that I could definitely help a patient who was suffering from a disease, which had *never before* been successfully treated, to prove the validity of my treatment. If such were, furthermore, well-documented and were witnessed by reliable observers, the verdict of science should not necessarily require the performance of a controlled study to verify its efficacy. Such, I admit, is the case with my "uncontrolled" studies of patients with alcoholism and other diseases, presented in the pages of this book.

Our first case study included a total of 22 patients who admitted having a definite and at times uncontrollable desire for alcoholic beverages. Characteristically, this desire appeared as a chronic problem which tended to be exaggerated by stress. Three of the 22 subjects suffered in addition to alcoholism, a concomitant problem with cocaine addiction.

Seven of the subjects were residents of *A Better Way In Christ Rescue Mission*, managed by J. C. Peace, who was himself one of the patients included in the study. The remaining 15 subjects were patients encountered in my every-day medical practice. Eighteen of the subjects were male, ranging in age from 21 to 82 years and with an average age of 62 years. Four were females, between 45 and 76 years of age and with an average age of 62. In all cases, each injection of niacin, after the first, was administered only after a careful, clinical appraisal of the possible effects of the previous injection and after appropriate adjustments in size and/or frequency of dosage were determined. Each patient was treated on an individualized basis.

Each subject received subcutaneous injections of niacin administered according to the principles in Individualized Replacement Therapy (IRT) described in my book on the subject. Most subjects received an initial dose of 5 mg of niacin. Subsequent injections were administered at intervals of two weeks or longer, depending upon the particular responses of each individual patient.

The results achieved were evaluated according to the following, admittedly overlapping criteria:

1. Direct statements by the subjects that they had noted a significant decrease in their desire for alcoholic beverages.

2. Observations by Mr. Peace that subjects who resided in his Mission were better able to cope with stressful situations without seeking relief through alcohol.

3. Observations by interested friends or relatives that subjects had been reducing their intake of alcoholic beverages significantly.

Twenty of the twenty-two subjects clearly benefitted from the injections of niacin administered in a precise, individualized fashion, according to the principles of IRT. Following are individual reports for each subject in the study. Subjects who were residents of *A Better Way In Christ Rescue Mission* are identified by an asterisk.

CASE REPORT #1
MALE *
AGE 46

This patient admits that he has been an alcoholic since 14 years of age and has drunk as much as two liters of vodka during a 24 hour period. At the time of his third visit, two weeks after having received 5 mg of niacin, he stated that he was able to control his desire to drink with less difficulty.

CASE REPORT #2
MALE
AGE 22

The subject had a problem with alcoholism for five or six years. He was hospitalized for it in Flint, Michigan, for two months in 1985. In the past, he has had an average consumption of up to twelve cans of beer daily and, more recently, four to six cans daily. He had also been taking cocaine for about two months. After his second five milligram injection of niacin, he was able to cut his beer intake down to two or three cans daily, a reduction of 50%. At the onset of his therapy, the patient stated that he consistently developed withdrawal symptoms two days after he stopped taking cocaine regularly. He discontinued taking the cocaine after receiving the first injection of niacin and did not resume it during the entire period of five months he was receiving niacin injections (5 mg) every two weeks. At no time during the course of observation did he describe any symptoms comparable with the effects of cocaine withdrawal he had experienced previously.

CASE REPORT #3
FEMALE
AGE 70

This patient's consumption averaged four to five cans of beer daily at the onset of her niacin injections. She reduced her intake of beer to three or four cans daily after her first injection of niacin (5 mg). She felt "much better" and had more energy. After the third injection of niacin (5 mg), she reported that she had not had any beer for a period of three weeks.

CASE REPORT #4
MALE *
AGE 36

The patient admitted he had had a problem with alcoholism for 19 years. Despite a chronic craving for alcohol, he had not had any alcoholic beverages for two weeks prior to the onset of his niacin therapy. He stated that he lost his craving for alcohol *within one hour* after the first injection of niacin. The craving did not recur for a period of ten days after the first injection and not at all after subsequent injections, which were given every two weeks over a period of three months.

CASE REPORT #5
MALE
AGE 21

This patient stated he had been drinking a six pack of beer daily for three years and had also been using cocaine on and off for two or three years. His desire for cocaine subsided completely after the first injection of niacin (5 mg) and had not recurred when he was last seen, four weeks after the second injection. He stated that he even refused an offer of cocaine. After his second injection of niacin, he reported that he had reduced his beer intake by 50%: from six cans to three cans daily.

CASE REPORT #6
MALE *
AGE 56

This man has a 32-year history of alcoholism. He periodically drank alcohol heavily, but had not been drinking since he was injured in an auto accident, three months prior to the onset of his niacin treatment. He was less depressed after his first injection of niacin, even though he was under great stress because he had been arrested for driving without a license and had had to post bail. He was able to avoid turning to drink, as he usually had in the past under such circumstances. After this patient's third injection Mr. Peace reported that the subject was continuing in the longest state of sobriety he had been able to maintain in the four years since he had been under observation at the Mission. The patient stated, "So far it is a miracle." He was still doing well when he was last seen, three months after the onset of the niacin injections of 5 mg, every two weeks.

CASE REPORT #7
MALE
AGE 40

At the onset of niacin therapy, this attorney stated he drank an average of ten to twelve cans of beer weekly. After his first injection of niacin, he noted a decreased desire for tranquilizers and for alcohol for a period of five days. He received a total of three injections of niacin, 5 mg each, at intervals of two weeks. When last seen, two months after his last injection of niacin, he stated that his craving for beer was definitely less than at the onset of therapy, and that he had not had any beer at all during the previous week.

CASE REPORT #8
FEMALE
AGE 57

At the time of her first examination, she admitted she occasionally drank alcoholic beverages "to excess." After her second 5 mg injection of niacin, she stated that she realized that she had a diminished desire for alcohol which lasted for two weeks after each injection.

CASE REPORT #9
MALE
AGE 49

This subject had an acknowledged problem with alcoholism for 24 years, and had been hospitalized between 30 and 40 times for acute alcoholism. Even though he was under much stress during the period following the first injection, he felt better able to cope without turning to the alcohol he would usually have felt a need for under similar circumstances. The patient had a similar experience after the second injection, when he had a serious family argument which ordinarily would, in his words, "throw me on the drunk." He also repeatedly noted a mild drop in energy for a few days before each dose of niacin, which would disappear within 24 hours after each of the 22 injections he received over a period of more than ten months. At first, he received five milligram injections, but it was soon found necessary to increase them to 5.6 mg each. Nevertheless, he did not have any alcohol at all during the period of more than one year which had elapsed between the time when niacin injections were started and the time he was last evaluated in June 1988.

It should be noted that this patient's case was discussed earlier in the text of this book. He is the author of the first two letters presented earlier in this chapter.

CASE REPORT #10
MALE
AGE 41

This physician, a certified orthopedic surgeon, found it necessary to close his office in August 1986, two years before the onset of therapy, because of alcoholism. He stated he was a "weekend drinker":

over those two days, he was in the habit of drinking a fifth of whiskey and a case of beer. When he returned three weeks after his initial 5 mg injection of niacin, however, he stated that he had noted a marked reduction in his craving for alcohol *within one hour* after the injection. He stated that he had no craving at all when he was seen at the time of this follow-up visit. He described transient symptoms of mild fatigue and over-stimulation after the first injection of niacin, lasting for about 10 days. These mild undesirable side effects did not recur when his subsequent injections were reduced by 10%, to 4.5 mg each time. His case is discussed further in the chapter on "A Mission of Mercy: 60 Miles to Deliver 4.5 mg of Niacin." It should also be mentioned that this doctor informed me that he had been treated without success at six different treatment centers before he came to see me.

CASE REPORT #11
MALE *
AGE 40

This subject had a known problem with alcoholism for about 20 years. Mr. Peace stated that this was the "most difficult" alcoholic in St. Lucie County. He had a history of being in and out of jail many times. Before he was given an injection of niacin he had a craving for alcohol which would come and go unpredictably. After a 5 mg injection of niacin, his craving subsided completely, and he experienced a marked improvement in his state of vitality and in his personality. His mind appeared to be awakening, and he participated in conversation in a way he had not done previously. The patient was aware of his improvement within two to three days. His testimony was corroborated by Mr. B. J. Kimbriel, a qualified counselor in alcoholism, who participated in our study. He stated the improvement he noted in this patient was "overwhelming."

CASE REPORT #12
MALE
AGE 31

This patient had a problem with alcoholism for eight years, which resulted in his confinement in jail on five occasions. After his fifth offense, his driver's license was revoked for the rest of his life. He noted much less of a desire for alcohol after the first 5 mg injection of niacin, and was also aware of increased energy and physical endurance. After receiving two injections of niacin over a period of four weeks, he stated that the smell of alcohol on a person's breath was repulsive to him. In his own words, "It stinks". After his fifth injection of niacin, on April 22nd, 1988, he stated "I feel that I am cured," and added that he no longer felt the need for additional injections. Arrangements were made to withhold any further niacin therapy unless he felt the need for it. When he was last contacted, by phone, on March 22, 1989, he stated that his desire for alcohol had not returned and that he still did not feel the need to resume niacin therapy.

CASE REPORT #13
MALE *
AGE 40

This patient experienced periodic drinking problems which occurred anywhere from one to twelve months apart, more frequently when he was under stress. The last such episode was one month before the onset of niacin therapy. As soon as niacin injections were started, he realized he was more relaxed and could cope with stress without turning to alcohol, as had been his practice in the past. He realized after the second injection of niacin that he no longer had any desire for alcohol.

CASE REPORT #14
FEMALE
AGE 45

    This subject had a problem with alcoholism for 6 years prior to onset of niacin therapy, drinking up to three bottles of wine daily. She was hospitalized twice for alcoholism, and took overdoses of sleeping pills on three occasions. She noted definite improvement within 24 hours after her initial injection of niacin, which was 6 mg. Her attitude was more positive and she soon lost her desire for alcohol. She continued to improve day by day, stating she felt "stronger" and was able to stay up later at night. During her period of improvement when she had received four additional injections of niacin, 6.5 mg each, numerous friends and relatives stated that they were highly impressed with her remarkable progress.

CASE REPORT #15
MALE *
AGE 26

In the past, this patient has had problems with beer, marijuana, cocaine and speed. Most recently, prior to the onset of niacin therapy, he had been excessively drinking beer for a period of 3-4 months. Mr. Peace reported that after the subject's initial injection of niacin (5 mg), he improved more rapidly than any of the other subjects under Mr. Peace's observation. He did not turn to alcohol, despite much stress, and his attitude was much more positive. The patient realized he had more pep and could cope with things better. After his second five milligram injection of niacin, he had at least two periods of definite stress and was able to cope with them without alcohol. On one of these occasions, he was caught by the police after a minor traffic accident and still did not feel the need to turn to alcohol. However, he complained of feeling "hostile" after the seventh injection, and consequently, further therapy was withheld while he was kept under observation. As he gradually lost his hostilities, niacin therapy was resumed, a total of 8 weeks after his previous injection. Upon resuming therapy, he was given an injection of only 2 mg of niacin, because it was felt that his last previous dose of 5 mg exceeded his therapeutic window. It should be noted that the 2 mg represents only 40% of his previous dosage. The patient began to improve within a few days, and improvement which was sustained. He continued to do very well on a dose of 2 mg administered every two weeks. Neither his desire for alcohol nor his hostility returned during the time he received a total of eight such relatively small injections.

CASE REPORT #16
MALE
AGE 82

This patient, a retired airplane designer, had a known problem with alcoholism since the death of his wife, seven years before the onset of niacin therapy. He estimated that he drank an average of 80 ounces of wine daily. When we checked him 20 days after the first injection of niacin, he stated that his wine intake had been reduced "by 100%". He also noted that he had more pep and vitality.

CASE REPORT #17
FEMALE
AGE 76

This subject was treated for acute alcoholism at Holy Cross Hospital in Chicago, from August 1-15, 1987. Treatment with niacin started in my office on August 27, 1987. After her first injection of 5 mg of niacin, she stated that she experienced less of a craving for beer. After receiving her fifth injection she reported that she had completely lost her desire for beer.

CASE REPORT #18
MALE
AGE 46

This patient admitted that he had been an alcoholic for 16 years and drank up to six cans of beer daily. Within 24 hours after receiving 5 mg of niacin, he noted a lessened desire for alcohol and reduced his intake by 50%, from six to three cans daily. Along with this, he reported an improvement in the efficiency of his daily work routine, and made fewer stops for beers on his bread delivery route during the course of the day.

CASE REPORT #19
MALE
AGE 41

This patient is a board-certified surgeon who knew he had had a latent problem with alcoholism since childhood, when his father, a physician, warned him that he might inherit the father's problem with alcoholism. As a result, the subject avoided an overt problem, because he was "on guard" when the tendency definitely began to appear as he grew up. He was, consequently, always able to control it, although his desire for alcohol remained.

As described in the Introduction, this patient responded very well to a series of three injections of niacin, each of 5 mg, given two weeks apart. As of April 10, 1989 his craving for alcohol had not recurred even though almost three years had elapsed since his third injection administered on July 22, 1986.

CASE REPORT #20
MALE
AGE 34

This patient is a well known, reputable surgeon who had had a known problem with alcohol for about eight years. For three years prior to the onset of niacin therapy, he also used cocaine. He stated that me more or less "got by" when he limited himself to alcohol, but after he began to use cocaine his condition steadily deteriorated. Finally he had to close his office for a period of nine months, from May 1986 to February 1987, in order to receive inpatient therapy for his addiction problem in another state. When his niacin therapy was started on February 27, 1987, he was under considerable stress because an impending divorce was expected in about two weeks, occurring after a separation of nine to ten months.

At the onset of niacin therapy, the subject estimated that his energy level was about 60% of what it should have been. After his first injection of niacin (5 mg) he developed a "terrible" pounding headache within 2 hours which lasted for about 4 hours. He could not recall having had a headache like this previously. Subsequently, he felt rather "anxious" for about 1 hour and felt somewhat more tired than usual for an additional 48 hours. After that time, he felt better than he had at the onset of treatment, a condition which lasted for 9 to 10 days. He began to experience an energy loss on the 11th day, at which time he was given a dose of 4.4 mg (12% less than the initial 5 mg dose). After the smaller dose, the patient did not develop a headache, but he did feel quite warm, starting about 1 1/2 hours after the injection, and the sensation lasted 2 to 2 1/2 hours. Subsequently, he felt quite well for 8-9 days, then once again began to sag a little.

The patient realized that, after the second injection, he felt less nervous, despite continued stress associated with his impending divorce. He also assured me that he definitely had more energy.

After receiving another reduced (4.4 mg) injection of niacin, this man felt especially well and realized that he had less of a desire for alcohol and cocaine under stress than he had previously experienced. He also noted that his energy level had returned to 100%. In addition, he did experience a slight drop in his energy level for the final 2-3 days before his scheduled two week follow-up visit.

This patient has continued to do well as the intervals between visits was gradually extended to every 6 weeks. However, we both observed that the effects of any particular injection tended to wear off to an undesirable degree if the interval between injections reached two months.

He was still doing well on April 3, 1989 more than two years after the onset of his niacin therapy and no longer had difficulty avoiding alcohol and cocaine completely. Not only that, he had expanded the scope of his medical practice to include nasal allergy, and moreover, informed me that he had not missed even one day's work since he started to receive niacin therapy in my office.

CASE REPORT #21
MALE
AGE 62

This man has been drinking an average of six cans of beer daily for several years when he started receiving niacin injections. There was no significant evidence that any of three injections of niacin curbed his craving for alcohol. He received a total of four injections of niacin; of 5, 5.6, 4, and 4 mg respectively.

The 4 mg dose of niacin was repeated because the first one of this potency was followed by transient subjective effects which suggested a diminution in a desire for alcohol. Unfortunately, no such effect appeared after the second.

This patient is necessarily classified as a therapeutic failure.

CASE REPORT #22
MALE
AGE 62

This patient had had a longstanding habit of drinking an average of five to six cans of beer daily before receiving any injections of niacin. There was no evidence that either of the two injections (5 mg and 6 mg respectively) curbed his craving for beer.

This patient is necessarily classified as a therapeutic failure.

Chapter Four

THE END OF THE RAINBOW IS IN SIGHT

ALTHOUGH FATHER TIME unerringly informs me that 52 years have come and gone since 1937, when I started as a medical student at the University of Chicago, I can still vividly recollect how my journey in the practice of medicine began. As I started, step by step, on that long, winding road, I vaguely sensed that it might ultimately lead me to some unidentifiable goal which lay well beyond the horizon bounding the scope of existing scientific knowledge at that time. I also realize that 1989 was the year in which the culmination of that journey, which at times has seemed endless, was reached.

I felt reasonably sure that culmination was definitely in sight as I wrote the opening paragraphs of the Introduction to this book, citing the challenging words of a reputable surgeon which unequivocally defy explanation in terms of all accepted ideas in the field of medical knowledge. Yet, with variations, I had heard similar renditions from 19 of the 21 subjects who received minidoses of niacin for their particular alcoholic problems.

When one of the last subjects of this study came along, I realized that the end of the journey must surely be in sight, for this subject gave me yet another report which seemed to defy all accepted medical ideas. Significantly, this individual was also a physician. He had traveled about 60 miles to see me on the recommendation of a nurse in Fort Pierce, who had told him of the results I had achieved in the the treatment of alcoholics. This new patient, a board-certified orthopedic surgeon, had found it necessary to close his office two years previously because of his problem with alcoholism and obviously needed help. At the time of his initial visit to my office, this physician was given a five milligram injection of niacin subcutaneously and was advised to write down in a diary, day by day, any changes he might note in the way he felt. When he returned for his follow-up appointment two weeks later, on January 11, 1988, he made the following statement: "My diary shows that I received the injection at 3:45 pm and, by 4:45 pm, my craving for alcohol had subsided considerably."

When I received this information, I realized that this was the twentieth success I had seen in twenty-two trials, indicating a "batting average" of 0.909 with IRT niacin therapy in my efforts to curb or dissipate a patient's craving for alcohol. Despite this high success rate, I know that the question may be asked by some readers as to whether or not this data can be considered scientifically acceptable, because no comparable series of "control" subjects were observed. Those who are familiar with investigative projects will recognize, of course, that such a question refers to the use of a group of twenty-two subjects who, without their knowledge, received "placebo" injections of salt water instead of niacin. In such experiments, it is implicitly assumed that, the demonstration of negative results is required before it can be concluded that any positive results achieved in the "experimental" group can be considered significant.

Although the use of a control group in experimental medicine has been considered a necessity by the editors of reputable medical journals for many years, I feel that there are valid reasons to question the need for such a procedure.

I intend to present systematically a series of reasons why I feel we have the right to question this requirement for "controlled studies" as a prerequisite for the inclusion of new therapeutic observations in a medical journal.

1. Such a procedure would immediately condemn as scientifically worthless any series of cases presented by a private doctor who does not have the financial resources to pay for study participants in any type of therapy who, knowing in advance that there was a fifty-fifty chance that they might only receive placebo injections, would probably require monetary compensation. After all, how many people could we reasonably expect to come in without some special inducement for such an experiment carried out by a private doctor who wants to find out whether or not some new form of treatment is of any significant value? From my own experience, and from my knowledge of psychology, I know that assembling a significant number of unpaid "control" subjects in a private doctor's office is next to impossible. Only in endowed research institutions can such studies be performed. A private doctor just does not have the time or the available funds to perform such studies. As a result, it is almost unheard of for any medical investigation of significance, which does not have

its origin in some major medical school or research institution, to appear in any medical journal. This automatically tends to stifle any efforts by private practitioners to engage in studies of possible scientific significance. Consequently, the private doctor's office can more or less be rejected as a source of new medical knowledge if prevailing attitudes regarding "controlled" studies persist. And this would, of course mean that my uncontrolled study of twenty-two patients, despite a batting average of 0.909, would necessarily be ignored by medical journal editors, and would thereby become unavailable to the many physicians who might otherwise benefit from it.

2. Let us consider the individuals, who serve as editors of medical journals and who are members of their editorial boards. They are necessarily physicians of the same caliber as the medical school professors responsible for the education of the medical students, who in turn will become the practicing physicians of tomorrow. These students, as has been shown in a previous chapter, receive an education, for the most part, which permits an overwhelming majority to become practitioners of empirical medi-

cine, which is based upon experience rather than science or theory. This is shot-gun medicine, based upon statistics which ignore the basic scientific law of cause and effect. I contend that the unscientific methodology of these practicing physicians is therefore to be laid upon the doorsteps of their teachers. And these teachers are the same men who dictate the editorial policies of "reputable" medical journals and must surely be in step with the typical medical school professors who make up their editorial boards.

Given the situation described above, I feel that I am entirely justified in questioning the basic structure of an educational systems which fails to recognize that it produces crop after crop of students who are basically unscientific in their every day practice of medicine and who continue to subscribe to medical journals which degrade original studies which are not adequately "controlled".

3. Next, let us consider a very basic question: Does every medical study have to be based upon controlled observations in order to have scientific merit? I believe I can logically prove that the answer, to this question is "NO!" First of all, we

must go back to the very basic scientific principle of cause and effect. To adhere to this principle, we must introduce only one new factor at a time into a problem situation, and then make observations with an open mind. Nevertheless, this scientific law does not require the parallel production of an artificial situation which simulates the experimental situation in question in order to eliminate the possibilities of dishonesty, prejudice, and suggestion. In other words, learned men implicitly assume that any true scientist who is adequately trained and experienced does not require a special maneuver in each of his experiments to make certain that his reported data are not influenced by the "human" inadequacies listed above. I contend that a competent, experienced, and well-trained scientist is, therefore, tacitly expected to be able to collect data which are not distorted by prejudice, dishonesty or wishful thinking. Therefore, I contend that I also have every right to insist that my educational background, including a B.S. from M.I.T. and M.D. and Ph.D. degrees from the University of Chicago, permits me the same exemption from the special maneuver of establishing a control group in order to make sure that the facts I present are obtained honestly and with an open mind.

4. Another way of looking at the problem is to realize that the net product of the educational system which follows this methodology, established by medical school professors and the journals to which they contribute and which they edit, has done little more than produce physicians who consistently fail to realize that they are fundamentally unscientific, and who profit not at all by their years of experience throughout entire life-times of practice.

I can only conclude from the above that the true scientific validity of any type of research project is not guaranteed by the presence of a "controlled" study, nor is it invalidated by its absence. Only the demonstrated competence and integrity of the investigator who has performed the study can offer such an assurance.

Chapter Five

A 60 MILE MISSION OF MERCY TO DELIVER 4.5 MILLIGRAMS OF NIACIN

A 60 MILE TRIP TO DELIVER 4.5 milligrams of niacin?

"Ridiculous"

"Absurd"

"Sheer nonsense"

Such responses could be anticipated with complete certainty from any physician, nutritionist, or other educated individual who had not heard of IRT. In no uncertain terms, such people could readily bring to our attention the well-known fact that there is no corner in the civilized world where there is anything resembling a shortage of niacin. After all, niacin tablets containing 100 milligrams, or even considerably more, can readily be purchased in almost any drug store in the United States.

What these people do not know, however, is that the niacin to which the title of this chapter refers was in the form of an *injectable solution*, and not as a tablet to be swallowed. I can further state that niacin in this injectable form is not available at this time to any physician in the United States other than myself. Sensitive to this fact, I have a supply of carefully stored vials of injectable niacin which I estimate is sufficient to fulfill my requirements for at least 10 years, even though I administer it to at least several patients in my everyday practice.

How I know that I am the only physician in the United States who has a supply of injectable niacin is probably somewhat puzzling to many readers, whose patience will be rewarded if they wait for the explanation of this enigmatic situation in a later chapter.

In the meantime, let us return again to the matter of a "Mission of Mercy to Deliver 4.5 mg of Niacin." Who has ever heard of using niacin, in any form, as a medical emergency measure? In urgent situations doctors are expected to use such items as oxygen, pain-killers, tranquilizers, antibiotics, and cardiac drugs. In other words, none of the well-known functions of niacin, a vitamin which causes flushing of the skin when given in relatively large doses, even suggests that it may be of any significant value in the prevention or the treatment of an emergency situation.

Before we go any further, let me mention that the emergency situation in question was that of a physician, an admittedly severe alcoholic, who had made a statement to me over the phone which strongly suggested that he might be contemplating suicide. From his home, in a community about 60 miles distant from Port St. Lucie, he had informed me that he had no longer had a desire to live. This followed in the heels of his admission that he was distressed because a judge had just awarded his ex-wife a large sum of money as part of a divorce settlement.

To understand why I immediately realized that he probably required an injection of niacin, containing exactly 4.5 mg, requires a careful review of the step by step analysis which led me to this mathematical solution to the challenging problem I have described.

As I proceed with this analysis, I feel confident in making the statement that no similar mathematical solution to a problem in medical therapy has ever been previously presented to the medical profession. I will further state, at this juncture, that the accuracy of the answer to this potential medical emergency is validated by the therapeutic results which were achieved and will subsequently be described. Needless to say, I feel that I can state with considerable confidence that few, if any, physicians, scientists or mathematicians who have not been exposed to the concepts of IRT, as presented in my previous book and in this sequel, could even attempt to make the analysis which follows. In other words, all currently accepted ideas in the field of medicine unequivocally fail to provide a solution to this problem. I further contend that they fail because medical therapy, as routinely applied by the majority of physicians, is based upon empiricism and not upon the scientific method. This has been discussed thoroughly in a preceding chapter entitled, "Is Medicine Truly a Science?"

Because most physicians do not care for patients who reside in locations as far away as 60 miles, most readers will probably have surmised correctly that the patient under discussion is the same physician whose response to an injection of niacin was presented in the previous chapter.

As was previously noted, this patient indicated that he had experienced a remarkably beneficial effect from his initial injection of niacin which he noticed within one hour: his craving for alcohol diminished considerably. Because of this excellent response after such a brief time interval, it may seem quite logical to repeat the same dose of 5 mg when he appeared ready for his next injection. Why, then, did I decide on 4.5 mg?

This minute difference in magnitude of 0.5 mg may seem even more preposterous than the dose of 5 mg the patient received initially, which was identical to the minute dose given to the physician described in the Introduction. Yet the reason for this minute dosage and its even more minute adjustment represents the fundamental principle upon which IRT is based. This is the optimal dose hypothesis, which is defined in my previous book as the concept that there is a therapeutic window which determines the magnitude of the dose of niacin required to produce ideal therapeutic results. This concept implies that doses which are below the level of the therapeutic window are inadequate, while those above the therapeutic window produce beneficial effects which may be preceded, accompanied, or followed by some adverse effects. Doses which are "on target," on the other hand, are followed by clinical improvement. Why then did we not repeat the dose of 5 mg, which appeared so dramatically beneficial? I did not do so because I found, after many years of methodical observation of thousands of patients, that it usually takes at least 10 days, and more often about two weeks, to make an accurate appraisal of the symptomatic effects of a physiological agent such as niacin. When I saw this doctor at a scheduled visit 14 days later, he reported that he had been somewhat tense, had been a little tired, and had periodically experienced excessive perspiration during the 10 days following the injection. Subsequently he did well and had little or no desire for alcohol.

From his description of the effects of the niacin, I was able to conclude that the initial dose of 5 mg of niacin was about 10% above this patient's optimal dose. In accordance with this, I administered a follow-up dose of niacin which measured 4.5 mg, a reduction of 10%. Subsequent to receiving this slightly smaller injection, the patient felt quite well during the entire interval and did not experience any of the transient undesirable side effects he had noted after the first injection. Nor did he experience any of such ill effects after another, later injection of 4.5 mg.

It therefore can be seen that I was confident that this doctor needed an optimal dose of niacin to help protect him from a resurfacing dependency on alcohol, a strong possibility while he suffered continual emotional stress. I also knew, from many observations under similarly stressful situations, that the beneficial effects of an injection given according to the methodology of IRT frequently did not last as long when the patient had been subjected to any great or prolonged stress. And I knew, moreover, that this patient had been carefully calibrated to a dose of 4.5 mg of niacin. That is why I was ready in advance to give him this precise dosage of the solution.

When I arrived at the patient's home with Mr. Peace, I was more than a little disappointed, however, for the doctor had obviously been drinking again. This could be seen by his confused and agitated behavior and by the partially emptied bottle of vodka in his room. I found it impossible to discuss his condition rationally with him while he paced about the room. Nor did I attempt to administer a tranquilizer. Instead, without delay, I inserted the planned 4.5 mg dose of niacin into a syringe and administered it to him subcutaneously. Within a few seconds, he said, "I feel itchy all over."

Soon, he began to smile and almost shouted "I feel wonderful," an assertion he repeated several times within the next few minutes. Then, without urging, he calmly sat down. Although he was incapable of intelligent discussion at the time, I felt that he was sufficiently relaxed and cooperative to merit my entrusting him to the care of his close friend, a retired criminologist, who was present at the time and who promised to phone me the next morning.

When I spoke to both of these people by telephone the next morning, I was able to conclude that the patient had spent a restful night and was once again in a state of normal mental clarity. And, particularly important was the fact that he did not have any craving for alcohol.

This experience, I fully realize, was unique, for I had evidently been able to demonstrate that a person who was suffering from acute alcoholism could manifest immediate and marked benefit from an injection of a pre-calibrated dose of niacin. The sequence of events which took place after he received this injection further indicates that the response was achieved without the use of any tranquilizer. I wish to emphasize this aspect, for I know, as a physician with more than 40 years of experience, that the usual treatment for a patient in this state of acute alcoholism would be the administration of an injection of a tranquilizer such as Librium or Vistaril, which I have given to a variety of patients under similar circumstances in the past. And at times, it was necessary to follow such an injection with a trip to the hospital emergency room. But this type of "standard" therapy was completely avoided by the prompt injection of the precise dose of niacin that I had previously determined was required to help normalize his body chemistry.

If my observations of the effects of niacin in this case of acute alcoholism can be duplicated by others, it seems entirely reasonable to conclude that this type of emergency therapy could represent a new and superior form of treatment for acute alcoholism. As an important prerequisite to its use, it would be absolutely necessary, of course, that each potential candidate for this therapy be precisely calibrated in advance to ascertain the exact dose to be administered at the time of an episode of acute alcoholism. In my office, it should be mentioned, I do this routinely, for I make a practice of administering IRT, in the form of niacin, to all patients who have any history of alcoholism. I do this because I have consistently observed, over the years, that the patients who have made any mention of present or past alcoholism will usually cope better and recuperate more readily from any type of illness if they receive injections of niacin. This particular aspect of niacin therapy is mentioned in my previous book on IRT, which cautions that this form of therapy may be worthless or even dangerous if one does not adhere meticulously to careful measures in order to achieve precise calibration in the case of each individual patient.

Chapter Six

NIACIN — THERAPEUTIC SUPERSTAR

*P*ROOF HAS ALREADY BEEN presented that niacin injections can help patients with alcoholism.

Do they help people who suffer from ailments other than alcoholism?

The answer to this simple question is a most emphatic affirmative, for niacin injections should unquestionably be classified as being of great therapeutic value in the every-day practice of medicine even though the medical community completely ignores their great potential in the treatment of victims of alcoholism.

First, it may be mentioned that the case studies described in this book included three subjects who were also addicted to cocaine, and who were helped in overcoming that addiction as well. I have two additional cocaine addicts as patients, who increase the number of cases to five.

A fundamental and consistent observation I have made is that this therapy helps restore and maintain a feeling of exhilaration and increased physical endurance in many patients who take their injections regularly. This is well exemplified in the case of my associate, Mr. J.C. Peace, whose case was presented in an earlier chapter. His repeated responses to injections of niacin given every two weeks for a period of over one year must be classified as truly remarkable. This seems especially true because his case report mentions that the magnitude of his injections had to be increased minutely, from 5.0 mg to 5.6 mg, in order to achieve consistently desirable therapeutic effects. The same remarkable effects have also been realized in patients who do not suffer from alcoholism as noted below.

Mrs. A.B., a woman of 62, came to me for care in January, 1985 because of recurrent anxiety accompanied by depression with a duration of about one month. She had a history of periods of anxiety dating back to her childhood and had been hospitalized for this in 1957. In 1976, she underwent several months of treatment with medication for hyperthyroidism. About three weeks prior to seeing me, she had gone to the emergency room of Port St. Lucie

Hospital because of what she described as vague, fleeting, incomplete thoughts which had started that day. At the hospital she received an injection of Haldol (commonly used for psychotic symptoms) and was advised to see a psychiatrist, which she did not do. In about two weeks her strange thoughts subsided, but she came to see me because she still was anxious and depressed. She also stated that she usually took two alcoholic drinks before dinner and had been a heavy drinker in the past. In addition, she stated that she had tired easily for many years.

Because Mrs. A.B. seemed rather sensitive she was given only 3.5 mg of niacin, 1.5 mg less than the usual initial dose of 5 mg. When I saw her again, two weeks later, she reported less fatigue, anxiety, and tension. Her subsequent clinical course is described graphically in the Appendix. The graphs illustrate the symptomatic fluctuations in her condition day by day and week by week over a period of 59 weeks. These graphs serve to exemplify the method of precise manipulation of timing and size of dosage which is required in the use of IRT.

As of June 1, 1988, it can be stated that this patient, who was incapable of tolerating regular employment at the onset of therapy, held a full-time clerical position at the local office of one of the largest business franchises in the state of Florida and is now the office manager, as of April 1, 1989.

This patient is fully aware of the size and timing of each injection of niacin and participates actively in making each analysis and hence any changes in therapeutic details. Review of her case must include the previously mentioned fact that she admits to having been a heavy drinker years ago, and this was an important reason why niacin was selected as the agent to use in her therapy. It is also interesting to note that the patient's optimal dose of niacin has changed very little over the period of two years since the series of graphs were completed on June 13, 1986. It should further be noted that she receives the smallest dose of niacin which I have found necessary for the achievement of therapeutic benefits in most patients, 1 mg. She receives injections, on the average, every two to three weeks. I must also repeat that no change in the size or frequency of dosage is made without definite confirmation by the patient, who usually suggests the specific changes which are made. After more than three years of therapy, there is no doubt that she knows as much about manipulation of her niacin as any intelligent and experienced diabetic knows about regulating his or her insulin injections.

Careful examination of the graphic representations of Mrs. A.B.'s case offers the interested reader an opportunity to observe the typical manipulations of dosage and timing which are necessary when IRT is administered. It should also be observed at this time that the same methodology is employed regardless of whether the patient has been receiving niacin or any other of the injectable vitamins or hormones customarily part of the IRT system of therapy.

After about 6 weeks of IRT therapy, Mrs. A.B. stated, "I feel much better than I have in a long time. I feel so much better that I am scared." In June 1988, more than three years after the onset of her therapy, the patient's husband informed me that the results he had observed from the niacin injections she had been receiving were "amazing" (see Appendix).

There are many other cases in which niacin IRT therapy produced remarkable results.

Mr. J.W., a retired man at 62 who suffered angina of effort due to coronary heart disease, consistently observed that his capacity to perform physical work increased greatly when he received injections of niacin (5 mg) every two to six weeks. His case was thoroughly described in my earlier book (see Reference 1).

Miss C.E., only 16 years of age, came to me for help because of an addiction to marijuana. In addition, she had a chronic skin affliction which had been diagnosed as psoriasis. After the first five milligram injection of niacin, her desire for marijuana diminished and she was able to reduce her average of 7 to 14 cigarettes weekly to 4 to 5 weekly. During this same period she noted that her skin condition showed significant improvement.

Mr. F.G., a 47 year old man and a former teacher of ballroom dancing, had a problem with chronic diarrhea for 13 years and had gone for help to two medical centers, the Lahey Clinic in Boston and the Thomas Jefferson Medical Center in Philadelphia. He was treated by six different physicians, but his diarrhea persisted. Because his initial five milligram dose of niacin had no apparent effects, his second dose, two weeks later, was increased to 5.6 mg. His diarrhea subsided completely after the larger dose and has not subsequently recurred during the seven months he has been receiving 5.6 mg every two weeks.

Mrs. J.K., a woman of 25 years who, despite her visits to a psychiatrist, had been unable to find significant relief from her agoraphobia. Her condition caused her to enter a state of panic whenever she was not in the company of her husband. This condition, however, improved steadily while she received injections of niacin (5 mg) every two to three weeks, over a period of seven months.

I believe that many readers with a basic knowledge of medical subjects will be puzzled by the fact that niacin was successfully used to treat so many conditions, none of which is usually considered one which can be helped significantly by this therapeutic agent. I know, for example, of no accepted medical textbook or journal which advises using niacin in the treatment of any of the medical ailments, described above.

Why then, have I experienced such success with niacin in these cases? I believe that a logical answer follows from an examination of available facts. A prime component is the group of basic symptoms which characterize pellagra, the disease which we rarely, if ever, encounter in 1989.

Pellagra, that almost forgotten ailment discussed in the Introduction, is characterized by the "Three D's," a medical mnemonic device which means "dementia, diarrhea, and dermatitis." These three symptoms are the hallmarks of pellagra, which occurred most commonly in people who lived in the "corn belt" of the United States and in a similar area in Italy. Typical diets of such people were almost exclusively maize corn, which contains little or no niacin.

When I considered these facts about ten years ago, I wondered whether pellagra was necessarily an "all or nothing" disease. Perhaps there were people who were only *partially* instead of completely deficient in this vitally necessary ingredient of their diets. Such people I thought, might have what might be a kind of "partial" pellagra, due to moderately deficient diets or inadequate absorption of niacin. If so, such individuals theoretically might be more susceptible to any of the "Three D's" because their tissue fluids contained a concentration of niacin which was less than ideal. It seemed logical that such people might be more likely than others to develop deterioration of the tissues of the brain, intestinal tract, and skin, a situation which would make them more susceptible to diseases affecting these tissues. As I continued thinking along these lines, it also seemed reasonable that such individuals might be helped by small doses of niacin, administered by the IRT system.

For about ten years I have been applying this hypothesis, and I feel the results I have described with the use of small niacin injections speak for themselves. I believe that I am now ready to make the statement that I have extended my partial deficiency theory even further, with successful results In the treatment of angina patients, such as the above mentioned case of Mr. J.W.

This newer aspect of my hypothesis takes into account the fact that large injections of niacin can cause flushing of the skin. Flushing is a direct result of the dilation of arteries leading to the parts of the body involved. This mechanism has been the basis of a method which has been used to improve the circulation of blood to the legs and to the brain: the administration of tablets containing large doses of niacin. Unfortunately, the results of this treatment have been somewhat disappointing, and it has consequently more or less been dropped.

When niacin is administered in small injections, by the IRT system, however, I have noted that this methodology diminishes significantly the frequency and severity of angina pain in many cardiac patients. Such results can be reasonably attributed to an improved flow of blood due to dilation of the coronary arteries which supply blood to heart muscle fibers and have been narrowed by disease.

It is important to mention that the patient reports discussed here represent only a few of the more outstanding and obvious results I have achieved with the use of niacin injections. I estimate that roughly 20% of my patients receive niacin injections regularly and are pleased to continue, because they note the consistently good results such therapy produces.

I should also mention that I have not yet included in this discussion any of the numerous observations I have made that injections of relatively large doses of niacin, approximately 100 mg for example, can be of remarkable benefit in the treatment of headaches. They appear to be effective in many headaches, regardless of the cause in each case. Relief may be noticeable within a few minutes, and it is especially gratifying because it makes it unnecessary for the physician to employ a narcotic drug such as Demerol or codeine. Similarly, I have seen dizziness abate in patients, regardless of the reason for its onset, within seconds of a subject receiving a 100 mg injection of niacin.

I also have preliminary data which strongly suggest that large injections of niacin may provide rapid relief to patients with acute asthmatic attacks. This has never, to my knowledge, been reported by others.

It should be noted that when niacin is used in such large doses, it acts more like a drug than like a vitamin; it does not react in a manner comparable to that seen when small doses are used, in accord with the principles of IRT. Instead, each large dose takes effect rapidly but may only last for several hours, comparable to the action of narcotic pain killers such as morphine or Demerol.

In a chapter devoted to niacin, it seems appropriate to bring to the attention of the reader the fact that I have noted that this vitamin, when used in small doses and according to the principles of IRT, has significantly helped at least one patient with the Duchenne type of muscular dystrophy, a disease which has uniformly been categorized as incurable. Below is a reproduction of a notarized statement from the mother of this patient, a young man from West Virginia. This lad had been under my care since August 25, 1986, and receives regular injections of ACTH as well as niacin. These are administered by a nurse, in accordance with instructions I give to the patient's mother during regular bi-weekly telephone interviews.

December 14, 1987

RE: William Ray Rose

To Whom It May Concern:

This is to certify that our son, William Ray Rose, has been under the care of Bernard D. Ross, M.D., since October 25, 1986 for muscular dystrophy of the Duchenne type. Both of us have noticed significant improvement in William's condition during the period of over one year that has elapsed since he has been receiving Individualized Replacement Therapy under the supervision of Dr. Ross.

We have noted the following specific indications of improvement:
 1. *He takes his boots off with less difficulty.*
 2. *Both of his arms are stronger.*
 3. *He has better control of the movement of his feet.*
 4. *He has a stronger grip in both hands.*
 5. *His teacher has noted that he can write more clearly.*

Mr. Claude Rose
Mrs. Brenda Rose

Below is a reproduction a notarized statement from another patient with the Duchenne type of muscular dystrophy.

Mr. & Mrs. Juan Szlachivk
2074 Oregon Avenue
Redwood City, CA 90461
November 23, 1987

Bernard D. Ross, M.D., Ph.D.
885 E. Prima Vista Blvd.
Port St. Lucie, Florida 34952

RE: Stanley Szlachivk

Dear Dr. Ross,

As the parents of Stanley Szlachivk, we are writing you this letter to let you know how much we appreciate the improvement we have observed in his general health as well as in his muscle function since he started to receive your treatment with injections of vitamin B12 and testosterone.

We have both noted the following types of improvement:

1. When lying on his back, he can now raise his forearms a total of 500 times, as compared to only 20 times before treatment was started in your office.
2. His speech is easier to understand because he now speaks more loudly and more clearly, due to improved action of the muscles of his mouth and tongue.
3. He needs less assistance with his meals.
4. He no longer feels exhausted when he returns home from school.
5. He has been achieving higher grades in school.
6. His facial contour has become more normal due to the fact that he has been closing his mouth more completely most of the time.

You surely know that we have been to other doctors who have been unable to help our son in any way.

Sincerely yours,
Mr. Juan Szlachivk
Mrs. Gloria Szlachivk

This patient, who resides in California, has shown remarkable and sustained improvement since he was started on IRT in my office on July 21, 1985. He receives injections of vitamin B12 and testosterone from his mother, again in accordance with instructions received from me during regular telephone monitoring. This patient, as well as Russell Libby (see letter below), provides evidence that IRT differs fundamentally from other forms of medical therapy because it employs specific therapeutic agents which are determined by the needs of the *individual* and not by the particular disease from which he is suffering. For example the patient, Russell Libby who resided in Fort Pierce, was helped by injections of ACTH and Adrenalin, while Robert Sharp, Jr. (see letter by Dr. Platzek) responded to injections of vitamin B12, testosterone, and niacin.

December 30, 1987

RE: Russell Libby

To whom it may concern:

I am writing as the mother of Russell Libby, who was under treatment for the Duchenne type of muscular dystrophy from

September 27, 1981 to November 17, 1984, a period of three years. When Dr. Ross undertook the care of Russell, he had been gradually getting worse, and I did not feel that he had long to live. He was wearing a diaper because of chronic diarrhea and poor control of his bladder. I had to bathe him and carry him around when he was not sitting in his wheelchair. All four of his extremities were involved to some extent and he needed assistance in eating his meals.

While on the treatment Dr. Ross administered, Russell gradually improved, as follows:

1. His chronic diarrhea subsided.
2. He had better control of his bowels and his urinary bladder and he no longer needed a diaper.
3. Sufficient muscle strength was restored to his arms and hands for him to engage in arts and crafts work and to make drawings, especially cartoons. He also became able to feed himself with less difficulty.
4. His attitude improved greatly and he went to school much more regularly. He graduated from high school and started college at Indian River Community College in Fort Pierce, Florida.
5. His chronic facial acne subsided.
6. His tendency to have almost constant bed sores subsided completely.

When he died of cardiac arrest on November 17, 1984, I reminded Dr. Ross that Russell had been going downhill steadily before Dr. Ross started treatment, and I felt that he did not have long to live. I felt thankful that the treatment Dr. Ross gave him provided me with three good years to enjoy his companionship.

Mrs. Paul Libby

NEUROLOGY CONSULTANTS
(A Partnership of Professional Associates)
1701 S. E. Hilmoor Drive • Building A, Suite 1
Port St. Lucie, Florida 33452

Bruce E. Platzek, M.D., P.A.
Darshan C. Aggarwal, M.D., P.A.
Susan C. Sult, Ph.D.

June 27, 1986

Dr. Neil Lewis
Muscular Dystrophy Association
810 Seventh Avenue
New York, NY 10019

RE: Robert Sharp, Jr.

Dear Dr. Lewis:

I am writing this letter at the request of Dr. Bernard D. Ross, who desires my opinion regarding the results he has achieved in the treatment of Robert Sharp, Jr., with a series of precise, individualized injections of various vitamins and hormones, which he terms Individualized Replacement Therapy (IRT).

From a review of old records obtained from the MD clinic in West Palm Beach, Florida, I learned that Robert had been suffering from the Duchenne type of MD since he was about two years of age. The diagnosis was first suspected in 1977 by Dr. L. Burton Parker of Orlando, when Robert was found to have a CPK of 7020. It was subsequently confirmed by Dr. Russell Wilson of West Palm Beach.

When he was last seen by Dr. Wilson in October, 1984, during the same month when therapy was initiated by Dr. Ross, he had the ability to extend and flex his wrists bilaterally, but virtually no other voluntary muscle movements could be observed. Dr. Wilson also reported that in the lower extremities Robert could merely wiggle his toes.

As a result of Dr. Ross' therapy, I was able, on August 30, 1985, to verify, to my own satisfaction, that Robert had shown convincing improvement in terms of a return of muscle functions which had previously been lost. He was able to comb his own hair for the first time in his life. In addition, it could be seen that his lower legs could move in a wide range of motion, although poorly controlled.

Sincerely yours,

Bruce Platzek, M.D.

BP/dsh

Based on the material presented in this chapter, I believe that any interested and open-minded reader will agree with my contention that the remarkable versatility of niacin as a therapeutic agent has at this time few if any equals in the entire realm of pharmacology.

Chapter Seven

**INJECTABLE NIACIN
IS NOT FOR SALE**

W HEN A NEW PRODUCT with demonstratable value and sales appeal is promoted for sale to the public, the manufacturer of such a product is protected by a patent which expires after a period of 17 years. During this 17 year period, no other company has the legal right to manufacture or sell the item.

But what happens if it is discovered that an old product, whose patent is already expired, is found to have remarkable value which has not been previously suspected? Even if it were obvious that the item could sell well when the reasons for its increased value become known to the buying public, the absence of a protective patent would constitute a marked deterrent to its manufacture and promotion by any company, despite the great potential of the product in question. The lack of patent protection would obviously permit all potential competitors to manufacture and sell the item long before the original company even had a chance to make enough profit to pay for its initial investment.

This happens to be the sad story with injectable niacin. I have known this item to be available for physicians to purchase for over 40 years; I am also aware that the patents for its manufacture expired many years ago. Unfortunately I also know, as a practicing physician who has been performing the experimental work with this vitamin preparation described in this book, that niacin's manufacture has been discontinued in the United States during the past few years. This is undoubtedly due to the lack of a demand for this item among the members of the medical profession, who do not even suspect that injectable niacin can produce any of the remarkable therapeutic results described in this and my earlier book on IRT.

In September of 1987, I had the opportunity to discuss this problem with an executive of a major pharmaceutical company. This individual stated that he was quite impressed by the results of my niacin therapy in patients with alcoholism, and that it is difficult to deny that IRT niacin represents a major medical development. Unfortunately, injectable niacin is still not for sale, and there is no immediate solution to the problem of its availability.

Fortunately, as I mentioned in the previous chapter, I have a supply of injectable niacin which is carefully packaged in sealed containers, away from exposure to light, and which should last for about ten years. In the meantime, I am pondering the problem of indentifying a practical means by which to make this safe and effective item available to other physicians for use in their every-day practice of medicine.

Epilogue

As they reach the end of this voyage of scientific exploration, I believe that readers of this book will have concluded that the American medical profession is a mass of contradictions. On the one hand, we have remarkable technological advances which seem to suggest a bright and promising future ahead. Eminent medical researchers, brought before us by the news media day after day, appear to be leading the way. However, the caliber of the medical care received by average people from average doctors leaves much to be desired. Evidence has been presented that patients frequently receive *empirical* medical care, which is essentially unscientific. Empirical therapy, characterized by a hodgepodge of multiple therapeutic maneuvers performed at one and the same time, is carried out with the fond hope that one or more of these measures will prove effective, as predicted by statistics. This cannot be classified as anything more than "shot-gun" therapy and fundamentally depends upon the oft repeated likelihood that 50% or more of all patients will probably get well, regardless of their ailments or the types of therapy prescribed by the doctor.

As long as they continue with this form of therapy, physicians cannot learn anything really new from their results in the treatment of any particular patient, because it is impossible for them to determine which specific therapeutic measure produced any significant benefit.

What can we do to remedy this situation? First of all, it seems necessary for medical educators to recognize the tremendous gap which exists between medicine as it is taught in medical schools and medicine as it is practiced every day in average doctors' offices. A simple and practical method which could resolve this problem would be a return to the "apprenticeship" system.

Ideally, medical apprenticeship could serve as a two-way system of communication. The practicing physician, by discussing typical patients with the medical student who is learning to share responsibilities in the office, could familiarize the neophyte with the problems he will later encounter in every-day medical practice. In exchange the student could relate, in like fashion, some of the newer aspects of medical knowledge to which he has been exposed in the classroom.

Necessarily underlying all this would be an unwavering dedication by all parties to the scientific principle of cause and effect. They would have to realize that it is illogical and unscientific to do more than one thing at a time unless practical circumstances demand it. Furthermore, in the event that such a compromise is made, the physician responsible must remain fully aware of his departure from scientific method and of the scientific circumstances which required it.

Finally, the author hopes that, somehow, teaching programs in medical schools will include measures to introduce students to the methods and principles of IRT, which the author contends is the most fundamental form of therapy conceivable at this time.

Let us reconsider a question posed earlier, in Chapter One: "What could be more fundamental that the individualized replacement of the exact ingredients which should be there in the first place?" So far, the answer to this question appears to be: "NOTHING." It must therefore be concluded, as of this writing, that the principles of IRT must necessarily take first priority when *any* form of therapy is planned in the treatment of any new patient. It does not matter whether the patient suffers from alcoholism, muscular dystrophy, heart disease, psychoneurosis, AIDS, or even lacks a definite diagnosis; what matters is that the basic principle of IRT is to assist the non-specific healing powers of the body to return to normal. It is with profound regret, therefore, that the publishers must state that Dr. Ross' contribution to the treatment of alcoholism will probably not be continued by anyone else, for we have no reason to believe that injectable niacin will be available again in the foreseeable future. As a result, Dr. Ross will probably never have the opportunity to teach other doctors to use it, even if they so desired. It seems highly likely that this method of treating alcoholism and other diseases with injectable niacin will die with him, unless...?

Appendix

*T*HIS SECTION PRESENTS to the interested reader a step-by-step explanation, using simple arithmetical terms, for each of the changes in the niacin dosage administered to Mrs. A.B., changes represented by the graphic curves shown below. It is important to realize that the same type of simple arithmetic is employed in an identical manner whenever one calculates the changes in doses required in the administration of any other agent used in IRT, regardless of whether it is vitamin B12, ACTH or anything else.

One problem which presents itself is the practical difficulty of preparing routinely such odd doses as 3.5 and 2.2 mg of niacin. This can be quickly overcome using a solution which is easily measured with acceptable precision in a standard tuberculin syringe and which contains ten mg of niacin per cc. Then, each cc of solution will equal 10 mg of niacin; a 3.5 mg dosage measures to 0.35 cc, 2.2 measures to 0.22 cc and so on.

It can be seen in the graphs that the first change in dosage occurs with the fourth injection, after the moderately severe adverse reaction, lasting about ten days, which followed after injection three. Injection three contained a dose of 3.5 mg which had previously given satisfactory results.

It should here be mentioned that adverse reactions resulting from overdosage during the use of IRT mainly manifest themselves in terms of aggravation of the very symptoms suffered by the patient before the onset of therapy. This has been discussed thoroughly in references 1 and 2 in the bibliography.

Since the duration and severity of the reaction to the third injection were quite significant, it was determined that a reduction of about 40% in the size of dose, down to 2.2 mg, was needed. When this decrement was found to yield satisfactory results, as after injections #1 and #3, this smaller dose was repeated until another adverse reaction was noted. This second negative reaction was quite severe and lasted, in an undulating fashion, for about eight days. It was then followed by gradual deterioration of the subject's condition which almost returned to the clinical level present at the onset of niacin therapy. Because of the severity of the initial phase of the reaction, and because the symptomatic state of the patient had deteriorated so significantly, it was felt necessary at this time to make the largest change in her dose made during the entire course of her treatment. This was a 45% reduction, from 2.2 mg to 1.2 mg of niacin.

The patient did well after the first of these smaller injections of 1.2 mg, but it should be noted that her condition showed a mild transient dip from 4+ to 3+ after the third injection of 1.2 mg. This was not follwed by any cut in dosage because it was felt that unusually severe stress at work was the probable cause of her minimal relapse. When on a subsequent date, however, she again showed a mild dip, her dose was lowered to 1.05 mg, which she continued to receive with evident benefit after a total of eight such doses.

During the ensuing period of two years and until this writing in April 1989 she has consistently received doses varying between 1.00 and 1.05 mg with continued success. Each time Mrs. A.B. comes in for her niacin injection, she informs me as to which of those two doses I should administer on that particular occasion. Most of the time during the past year, the dose has been exactly 1.00 mg, the smallest dose of niacin I have ever administered to any patient.

Results of IRT Using Niacin in Woman with Depression, Fatigue, Anxiety and Psychotic Symptoms

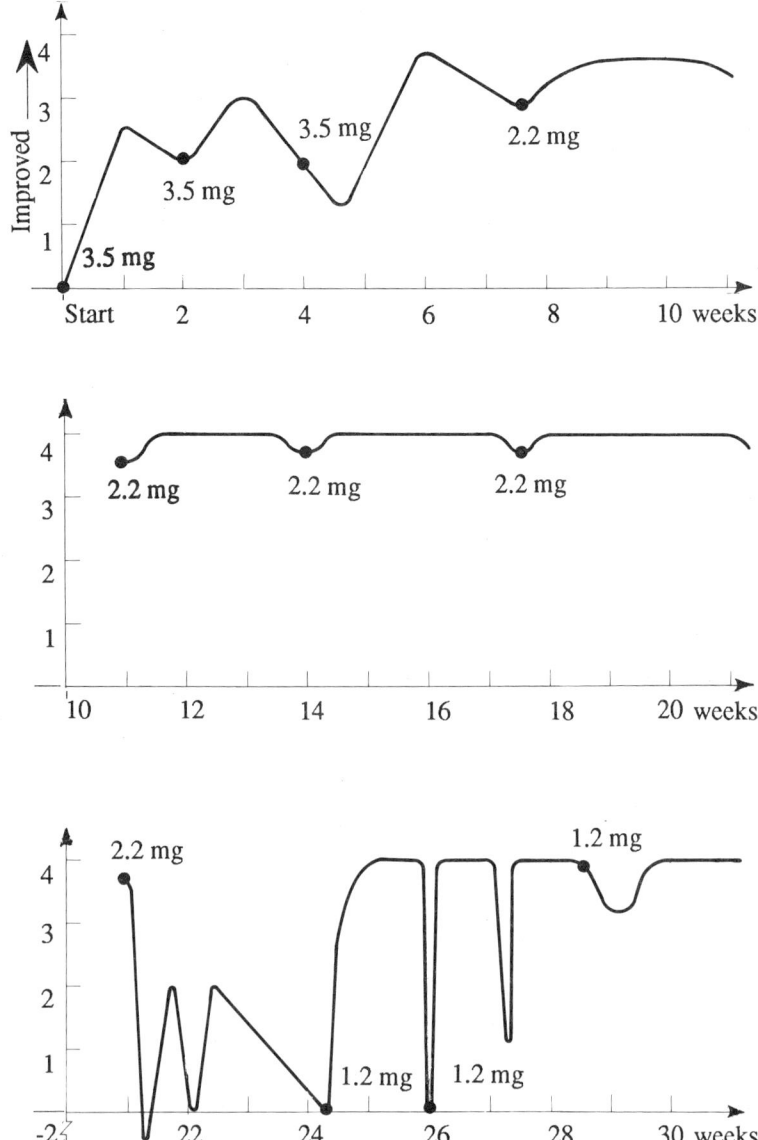

Improved
4
3
2
1
1.2 mg
1.2 mg
1.05 mg
1.05 mg
30
32
34
36
38
40 weeks
4
3
2
1
1.05 mg
1.05 mg
1.05 mg
40
42
44
46
48
50 weeks
4
3
2
1
1.05 mg
1.05 mg
1.05 mg
1.05 mg
50
52
54
56
58
60 weeks

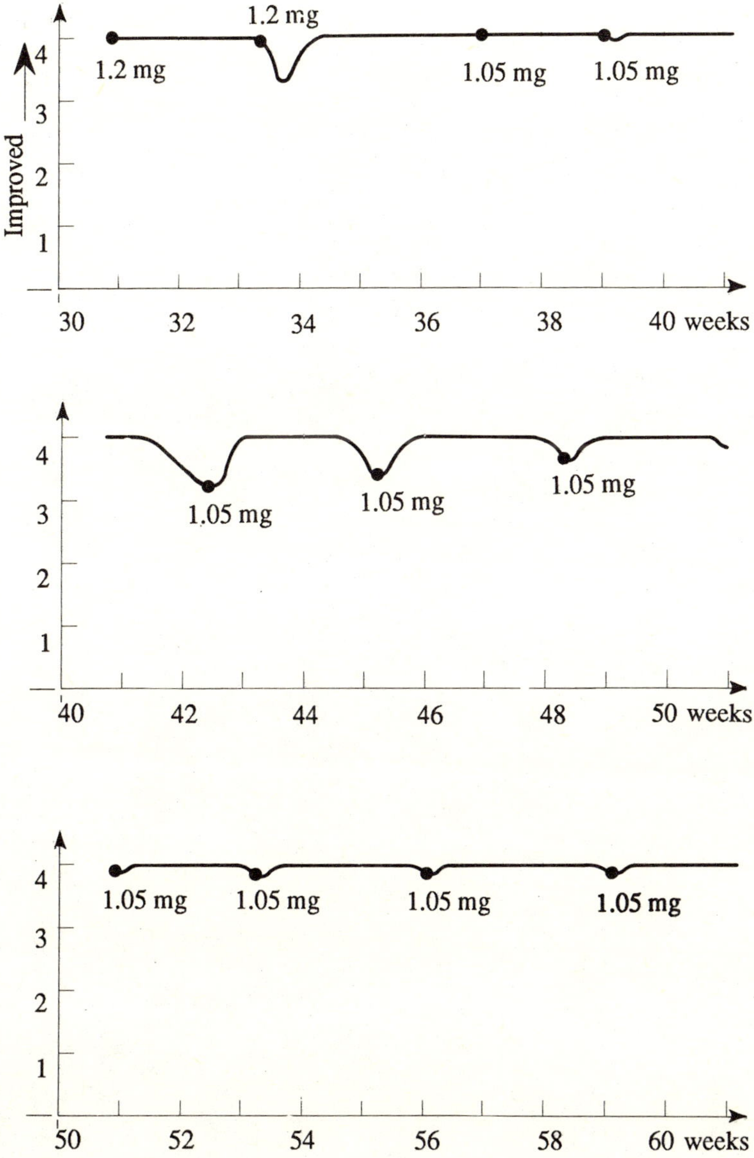

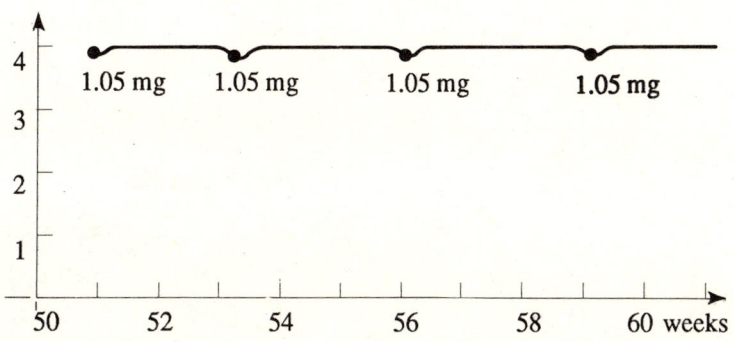

Bibliography

1. Ross, B.D., *The Fundamental Pathway to Better Health*, Book Publishers, Inc., Tampa, Florida, 1984.

2. Ross, B.D., and Ernst, G., *The Use of Vitamin B12 in the Syndrome of Non-Specific Hepatic Fatigue, a Common Condition Simulating Psychoneurosis*, Acta Neurovegetative, Wien, Bd IV, Heft 1, pp.73-91, 1952.

3. Payer, L., *Medicine in Three Countries: France*, M.D., v. 30, pp. 115-117 and 172-175, 1986.